Prior Park
Landscape Garden
BATH

A souvenir guide

C000149723

THE NATIONAL TRUST

Above Ralph Allen
(1693–1764) by John Faber Jr,
after Thomas Hudson

ONE MAN'S CREATION

Prior Park is chiefly the work of one man – Ralph Allen, an entrepreneur with a concern for improving not only his own situation but also the way the world worked for and looked to others.

Posting a letter in the early 18th century was an act of faith. The route your letter would take could be long, passing through many different hands, not all of them honest. There were just six post roads serving the country, all operating out of London. The system was open to abuse at several different stages. In 1711 an Act of Parliament was passed in an attempt to improve the situation, increase the number of routes and provide revenue for the government.

This was the system when Ralph Allen was appointed Postmaster in Bath in 1712, aged just 19. Born and raised in Cornwall, he was familiar with the postal business: his grandmother and then uncle had run the post office at St Columb, an important office at that time. Allen's business acumen coupled with tact and diplomacy would ensure his success.

Allen had been living close to the centre of Bath in a substantial dwelling still known as Ralph Allen's Town House, and in 1735 he moved to Widcombe to the south, just over the river. But his sights were set higher.

Bath stone

For hundreds of years good-quality stone had been quarried and mined from Combe Down, south of the city. Bath was rapidly expanding and becoming a fashionable place to stay, take the waters at the new Pump Rooms and generally be seen.

This was the second business opportunity Allen spotted and, with the same mix of organisation and determination, he made his second and larger fortune. By treating workers well and employing the latest techniques, he bought several mines and combined them into an operation capable of handling thousands of tons of stone. What was needed was a means of transporting the stone over the mile or so from the mines to the city below.

At that time a new invention was gaining in popularity – the railway. Allen commissioned one to be built along a track from Combe Down to the River Avon where the rough stone could be worked for use in Bath or sent to Bristol. Another of his business ventures

Above The wharf on the Avon, showing Allen's railway and two rows of workers' cottages; Buck's view of Bath, c.1734

Allen's fairness in the treatment of workers was typical of the man but also made good business sense. John Wood the Elder wrote: '*It was resolved that Houses should be erected on the top of the Down, for all such as should be concerned in Digging, Raising, and transporting the Unwrought Stone down to a common Yard by the Water Side; and that the Masons employed in Working it should have proper Sheds in that Yard to Work under, as well as Houses near to Live in: In Pursuance of this resolution I made Designs for two small Towns to receive the two Sets of People thus to be employed.*'

was to make the River Avon navigable between the two cities, thus allowing stone to be used in Bristol as well as exported around the coast to London.

The price of the stone actually came down as a result of this efficiency from 10 shillings to 7s 6d per ton but, because the quantities involved were so huge, Allen made a great deal of money.

A new mansion

The stone was selling well in Bath and Bristol but Allen was keen to see it used further afield. Some did find its way to London, being used for St Bartholomew's Hospital around 1730, but it was always seen as inferior to the harder Portland stone. This seems to have been one of the spurs that compelled Allen to show the world just what the stone was capable of.

He was already having dealings with John Wood the Elder, the architect of many of the splendid new buildings in the city, so it is not surprising that Allen turned to him to realise his ambitions. The new mansion was dramatically sited, not quietly tucked away in a valley, but perched high in order to command views out and admiration back.

The style would be Palladian but on a scale and grandeur to set it apart. With its flanking pavilions, it would be the longest in Britain at the time. Carving both outside and in would be of the highest quality – proof that Bath stone was second to none. Wood's design was based on an earlier, unbuilt example from *Vitruvius Britannicus*, its curving front emphasising the theatricality and prominence of its siting on the slope.

Above Prior Park in 1752; engraving by Anthony Walker. Curious visitors look over the wall into the informal Wilderness, which contrasts with the more regular planting to the left of the central lawn. The railway on the right brought blocks of Bath stone from the Combe Down quarries to Prior Park and the riverside wharf at the bottom of the valley

A SHIFT IN THE LANDSCAPE

18th-century gardens were packed with an eclectic and radical mix of aesthetic values, historical symbolism and political beliefs. This was a time of classical temples, shell-covered grottoes, ruined Gothick temples and artificial cascades. Gardening luminaries mingled with the artists and politicians of the day, informing the landscape movement.

Above Alexander Pope (1688–1744) was a frequent visitor to Prior Park

Right Pope in his Twickenham grotto, sketched by William Kent

One eminent influence at Prior Park was Alexander Pope. He travelled extensively in England, enjoying the hospitality of patrons such as Lord Bath at Cirencester and Lord Burlington at Chiswick. He was amongst other guests at Prior Park that made up a clique of cultured individuals welcome in the splendid mansion and its surroundings. Others included the author Henry Fielding, William Pitt the Elder and the actor David Garrick.

In *Epistle IV* addressed to Lord Burlington, Pope exhorts:

Consult the genius of the place in all;
That tells the waters or to rise, or fall;
Or helps th'ambitious hill the heav'ns to scale,
Or scoops in circling theatres the vale;
Calls in the country, catches opening glades,
Joins willing woods, and varies shades from shades,
Now breaks, or now directs, th'intending lines;
Paints as you plant, and, as you work, designs.

Pope died in 1744 but his influence lived on. The addition of the Palladian Bridge in 1756 altered the whole shape and scope of the landscape. The early formality shown in Anthony Walker's engraving of 1752 is gradually softened and a new perspective was achieved by building the bridge.

Major work was carried out to enlarge the existing ponds. By the creation of dams the water was captured in three lakes and from the mansion they appear as a single sheet.

Thomas Robins' pen and wash sketch of 1758 shows the bridge and a central cascade, with the upper pond still intact. There is some

debate as to whether this cascade ever existed, as archaeological investigation has failed to detect any trace of it. Robins produced many illustrations for wealthy patrons during this period, some of which may have been proposals rather than sketches from life. What is interesting is the transition from the early formality, still visible near the mansion, to the more natural appearance of the Lakes below.

By 1762 the Thorpe & Overton survey plan shows the whole scene united down to the bridge, the woodland edges are curved and, in the south-west corner, the Wilderness has retained a distinct, intimate character.

The Brown mystery

There is a bit of a mystery concerning the involvement of Lancelot 'Capability' Brown at Prior Park. By 1760 he was helping to shape the landscapes at Longleat, Corsham Court, Newton St Loe and Bowood, all within a few miles of Bath. It is recorded that Allen paid Mr Brown the sum of £60 for '... surveys and making plans at or about Prior Park'. The account was not cleared until after Allen's death in 1764 and, according to the Thorpe & Overton plan of 1762, the garden had reached its final stage of development. Either the payment was late and Brown did plan the major works to extend the lakes, position the bridge and sweep away the earlier formal scheme below the mansion, or Allen was seeking advice for another of his many holdings around Bath.

Whatever the case, Prior Park remains a fine example of landscaping, making full use of the dramatic site and contours. The 'hanging' woodlands on either side of the valley are typical of Brown, and the whole meets with Pope's exhortation: 'In all, let *Nature* never be forgot.'

Above A pen and wash sketch by Thomas Robins in 1758

Below Thorpe & Overton's map of 1762

Neglect

This was the stage the landscape had reached by the time Allen died in 1764, and in the years that followed not much changed. There was no direct heir and the estate was sold several times. The mansion was first a seminary and later became a Roman Catholic public school, which it remains today. It has suffered two major fires, the last being in 1991.

Following years of neglect there was considerable degradation to the buildings, whilst in the Park seedling ash, sycamore and bramble grew up and laurel ran amok. The Serpentine Lake was mostly filled in and the whole place had a feel of romantic decay. This was the situation when the National Trust acquired the garden from the Christian Brothers in 1993.

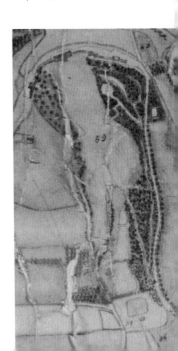

ROMANTICISM REBORN

The National Trust has embarked upon an ambitious programme of restoration. It is the appearance that the garden had reached by 1764, when Ralph Allen died, that work at Prior Park has been directed toward.

Since acquisition in 1993, research and understanding of 18th-century landscape gardens in general and Prior Park in particular have revealed its full significance. Apart from what is immediately discernible on the ground, the next step in garden restorations is to have a look underneath. Informed by records like old maps, plans, contemporary accounts, illustrations and archival evidence, archaeology can reveal many things – and also raise many more questions.

From the start of Trust ownership, archaeologists have been building up a picture of how Prior Park looked in the 18th century. Things are fairly straightforward here because after Ralph Allen died in 1764 the garden was neglected; buildings decayed, seedling trees and shrubs grew, and lakes silted up. There were no subsequent owners to develop things in the intervening years. Often in gardens it is these layers of influence that lead to questions of which features are worth saving and which may be sacrificed for the sake of a historic restoration. It should also be said that few historic gardens are exact replicas – processes of growth and decay see to that. Gardens are living, breathing things that are constantly changing.

First things first
Before the garden could open to the public a few essentials were needed. The circuit walk was blocked by overgrown laurels and brambles, many trees were unsafe, and some basic amenities were required. A team of volunteers cleared the pathway, tree surgeons made trees safe, and an entrance kiosk and toilet block were built. The circuit walk was laid with a new surface using locally quarried stone brash (waste from quarrying). This work, along with the repairs to the bridge and dams, took place before 1996 when the garden first opened to the public.

There was also an early debate as to how visitors' cars might be accommodated. It soon became apparent that there was just not enough room for a car-park on the 26 acres given to the National Trust by Prior Park College. This problem was resolved by the decision to not have car parking, but instead encourage people to arrive by public transport or on foot. Prior Park is happy to be still operating this scheme today when the reduction of car use has become an imperative.

Opposite The Palladian Bridge in 1946 showing the lower lake overgrown with reeds

Left One of the lakes being re-puddled in 1994

A WALK IN THE PARK

Landscape gardens were created to stimulate the senses. The circuit walk guides the visitor to the best views and features. Within a natural, idyllic landscape, temples and grottoes were placed to create scenes of beauty and grandeur. You can enjoy much the same experience today: just take a bit of time to relax into your immediate surroundings and let the path (and this book) be your guide.

THE WILDERNESS
This discrete corner of the garden retains a character of its own. Through all the changes that occurred in the valley to the Lakes, the Wilderness continued to develop the feel of a more cultivated garden. They were anything but wildernesses as we understand the term today, with winding paths flanked by flowering shrubs leading to architectural features and dark retreats.

Below Sketch by William Kent of Pope's garden at Twickenham, showing Miss Bounce's father

A short detour is worthwhile from the entrance kiosk along the driveway to the Grotto remains.

Mrs Allen's Grotto

Alexander Pope was particularly keen on these curious structures and built an elaborate one at his Twickenham house. Refuges from the open, they would have been places where interesting rocks, minerals and fossils could be shown off. An account comes from a student who attended Bishop Baines Seminary, located in the mansion, in 1836: 'The roof and sides of this sweet retreat presented to the eye such a dazzling assemblage shells, fossils, minerals etc as perfectly astonished us. ... The floor was almost as beautiful as the roof, being composed of a curious kind of stone perforated and inlaid with pine cones, fragments of bone etc, arranged in tasteful forms and the whole place exhibiting such a profusion of ornament and such a combination of taste and skill as I had never before witnessed.'

From the elaborate structure described here, the Grotto suffered during the years of neglect to the extent that, when the National Trust acquired Prior Park in 1993, all that remained above ground was a broken archway. Archaeologists found the floor under layers of leaf mould, with about half of the fossils, pebbles and bones set into it.

A Great Dane dog named Miss Bounce was given to Allen by Pope, and when she died she was buried under the floor. An epitaph was inscribed on a stone slab: 'Weep not, Tread lightly my grave, Call me Pet'.

As a temporary measure, to protect the remains, a tin shed has been erected over the whole site and both the protection and presentation of the Grotto will be improved when funds permit.

Retrace your steps to the entrance kiosk and turn right down the path. When you are behind the kiosk turn right.

Below The floor of the Grotto is encrusted with rare minerals from Cornwall and is made of pebbles, bones and ammonites

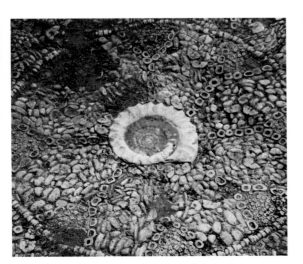

9

The Serpentine Lake and Sham Bridge

The Serpentine Lake was restored in 2006/7 with a grant from the Heritage Lottery Fund. Extensive archaeology soon after acquisition revealed the lake's original stonework. A formal, straight-sided canal was modified to create a more natural shape in about 1740. Its position is not natural however, perched on the side of a hill. Substantial retaining walls were built as well as a system of culverts to direct natural spring water from the slope into the lake.

The restored lake has given the Sham Bridge its original purpose back, as a termination that suggests water beyond. This structure had also suffered over the years and stonemasons made a fine job of recreating the vermiculation (wormlike carvings) of the pediments.

Bath stone was used in the restoration, which will weather and soften. Careful introduction of water plants keep the water healthy, giving clear reflections of the mansion and Sham Bridge.

Just beyond the Sham Bridge, turn left down some steps and walk along to the Cabinet.

Above The Serpentine Lake and Sham Bridge

Below A mason recreating the vermiculation on the Sham Bridge

THE WILDERNESS

The Cabinet and Cascade

This circular expanse of gravel was known as the Cabinet, an unusual use of the term meaning an outdoor 'room'. In the mid-18th century, cabinet could refer to a room full of cabinets for the display of curiosities. The feature can be clearly seen on the Thorpe & Overton plan of 1762 (see page 5). It was intended to restore the Cabinet with a grass surface, but during the excavations a clear layer of gravel became visible and the Trust decided to reinstate this surface. This is an example of being willing to change direction in the light of new evidence.

The structure of the Cascade required much investigation leading to careful rebuilding. At the top, where the water overflows from the Serpentine Lake, a series of carved grooves showed that there was a system of weir plates for holding the water back, but also giving the possibility for a sudden release or 'gush' over the Cascade. Under normal operating conditions, water from the lake simply overflows onto the Cascade. To create a gush, a weir plate is raised allowing more water out. The Cabinet was probably an area where guests would assemble to witness such a spectacle, no doubt expressing their delight with gushings of their own.

After flowing over the Cascade, the water is fed into a pipe under the Cabinet, reappearing in front of the site of the Gothic Temple. It then joins an elaborate series of culverts which carry it underground to the upper lake above the Palladian Bridge.

Left The Cascade in the Wilderness

By the 20th century the temple was in a sorry state and was finally sold in 1921. It was moved, stone by stone, to a private garden about a mile from Prior Park, where it still stands. The National Trust very much hopes to build a replica of the Gothic Temple on the original site. It is possible that trainee stonemasons attending the building construction course at Bath City College will use it as a training exercise. At the time of writing we are still working out the details of such a partnership. Bath stone, still being mined nearby, has been offered free of charge if the project comes to fruition.

Follow the path which goes to the right on the far side of the Cabinet.

Site of the Gothic Temple

The site where this small temple stood can be clearly seen on the ground. This was one of the later additions to the garden built around 1754 in the Gothic style. Ralph Allen was experimenting with a different style of architecture, free of the influence of Alexander Pope who died in 1744. As can be seen from the illustration, the Temple was elaborately carved, Allen again showing off the qualities of Bath stone.

Retrace your steps across the Cabinet, back up the steps and out of the Wilderness to the Mansion Viewpoint.

MANSION VIEWPOINT

'This house is acknowledged to command perhaps the finest view in the kingdom; and from its lofty situation, the magnificence of its portico, and its general appearance, affords splendid object to the city of Bath and its environs.' John Collinson, 1791

The mansion dominates the simple sweep of the valley down to the Palladian Bridge, village buildings of Widcombe and the city beyond. Allen's first scheme for the garden was more formal and the whole terminated about half way down at a circular pond (see Anthony Walker's engraving of 1752 on page 3).

The woodland margins on either side are a similar shape to those shown in the Thorpe & Overton survey map (see page 5). The whole scene must appear much as it did after the bridge was built in 1755. The city has changed though. In the early 18th century little expansion had taken place outside the old walls, and development to the east did not come about until Pulteney Bridge was built in 1769. Many of the buildings in the foreground date from the 19th and 20th centuries.

From up here the Lakes appear as a single sheet of water disappearing around the corner as if a river. Take time to enjoy the view. At different times of day and weather conditions the scene is ever-changing. For a view of the whole city, take the Priory Path described shortly.

Follow the path to a point on the downward slope where it splits. The recommended route is to follow the path to the right, the Priory Path, to the second viewpoint. It is uneven in places and can be slippery in certain conditions. The main circuit path continues on.

'A noble seat which sees all Bath and which was built for all Bath to see.'
Philip Thicknesse, 1788

'This is still one of the finest urban landscape views in the world.'
Sir Patrick Abercrombie, *A Plan for Bath*, 1945

Opposite Cows in the pasture in the valley of Prior Park Landscape Garden

PRIORY PATH

This path wends its way through a leafy glade full of a succession of snowdrops, daffodils and wild garlic in their seasons. The view of the city is well worth the detour.

Summerhouse Glade to Fishponds Cottage

The Priory Path leads to a small summerhouse tucked away in the trees. This charming little building remains a bit of a mystery. It is likely that it formed part of the farm buildings which were situated across Ralph Allen Drive – the farm was sold to developers in the early 20th century. This building was moved to the present site in around 1912 and the photograph below shows men carrying out the rebuilding work. The area seems to have been gardened at this time, perhaps by senior masters who lived in the Priory House visible through the trees. Further evidence of this is a small pond and some ornamental planting.

When the National Trust acquired Prior Park in 1993, all that remained of the Summerhouse was the timber frame. A specialist craftsman recreated the roof using Cotswold stone, but the rest was carried out by

Right Wild garlic cascades down the banks below the Priory Path

Trust staff and volunteers. Wood for the cladding came from an oak tree that had fallen nearby. The photograph from 1912 was very useful for showing us how it originally appeared, and it was posed again with two of the staff and two volunteers who were much involved in the rebuilding.

Continue up the steps and out into the field to the second viewpoint.

The photograph that was so instrumental in the reconstruction of the Summerhouse was donated by a local man and grandson of the impressively moustachioed gentleman who stands second from left in the original grouping.

BATH VIEWPOINT

Many well-known Bath buildings can be picked out from this vantage point, including the Royal Crescent, the Abbey and Pulteney Bridge with the weir in front of it.

Although the Priory Path was not part of the original layout, it was created to bring the visitor to this spectacular view of the whole city of Bath. Circuit walks within landscape gardens would often lead to views of what was known as the 'borrowed landscape'.

The surrounding fields are owned by the National Trust and form part of a 500-acre holding which protects much of the country-side on the south-eastern slopes of the city. They are managed for their diversity of wildlife habitat, considerable landscape value and public access.

Continue along the path and down steps to a kissing gate. Down some more steps, rejoin the main path and turn right.

Fishponds Cottage

The path descends steeply between banks planted with ferns to some tall yew trees and shrubberies either side of the path. On the Thorpe & Overton survey plan of 1762 buildings can be seen here, but it is uncertain as to whether the present cottage dates to this period.

A range of trees and shrubs has been planted in a 'theatrical' style, ranked steeply from low-growing periwinkle by the path, through hypericum, rubus, roses and viburnum, to cherry, arbutus and cercis at the back. Roe deer regularly browse here and carry out their own style of pruning.

Opposite · **Left** Guelder rose (*Viburnum opulus*) in autumn
Right Lesser periwinkle (*Vinca minor*)

Below The Bath Skyline

For visitors leaving the garden here, use the gate near Fishponds Cottage. However, a walk around the Lakes and to the Palladian Bridge is recommended before leaving. Also nearby is a small tea kiosk which serves refreshments at weekends between March and October and during school holidays.

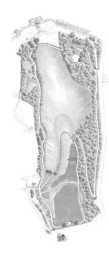

THE LAKES

There are various routes around the Lakes giving fine views back up to the mansion. The Lakes support a diversity of wildlife and an ice house can be discovered on the west bank.

Once beside the Lakes it can be appreciated that they are not the natural features they appear from the viewpoint at the top of the garden. Major work was carried out to create them: three dams were constructed including one under the mighty Palladian Bridge. By 1758, when Thomas Robins sketched the scene (see page 5), the bridge is built and dams have harnessed the water into the Lakes we see today.

Enlivened by ducks, herons, swans and the occasional kingfisher, the water supports associated wildlife. Carp swim lazily, feeding on the bottom. There are ongoing problems with leakage, only to be expected with features designed and created some 260 years ago.

It is worth going down to the bottom dam to get the view back up to the mansion with the bridge spanning the water. At a point as you approach the bridge, the mansion appears to sit on top of it.

The Ice House

A short diversion up the path at the end of the middle dam leads to the Ice House. This is an unusual example, being a long way from the mansion. Ice would be cut during severe winters, stored between layers of straw in the underground chamber and used in summer. It was used in specially designed food stores rather than for putting in drinks. Before refrigerators it was a sign of great wealth and some pride to have a source of ice in summer.

Beside the path, adjacent to the Ice House, the site of a building can be seen. This was an octagonal thatched house which can be seen on the border of the Thorpe & Overton plan (see page 5). It may have been used in conjunction with the Ice House – a shady retreat in summer months or simply an ornamental entrance.

The Palladian Bridge

This classical structure has a dam beneath it and spans the water in an elegant stride. Built in 1755, it shifted the whole focal point down the valley and serves as an eye-catcher as you walk around the garden.

This was the last of a series of such bridges built in England, the others being at Wilton (in 1735) and Stowe (in 1738). There is a fourth in St Petersburg, Russia. Richard Jones, Ralph Allen's clerk of works, is credited with getting the Prior Park example built. The design differs from the other two, and it has been suggested that Thomas Pitt finalised it – he was the nephew of Allen's friend William Pitt. From the top of the garden, it is a focal point in the landscape as a whole. Up close, it is a structure to be entered and enjoyed. The National Trust undertook major restoration work between 1993 and 1995, and it was completely re-roofed using Cornish slate, a nod towards Ralph Allen's origins.

The smallest lake is above (south of) the bridge and was completely silted up by 1993. At the far end, water, picked up from both sides of the valley and fed into a central culvert, is finally discharged. Tons of silt were removed, the lake re-puddled with clay and the banks re-profiled. A silt trap was also constructed to prevent similar problems in the future.

Above A view through the loggia of the Palladian Bridge

Several features on the bridge itself were restored, including parts of the balustrade and some of the ball finials which were discovered in the mud below. The temptation to blast off the stonework was resisted and a light touch applied instead. As a result much graffiti remains, some dating back to the late 18th century.

Above The design of the Palladian Bridge is from that of Andrea Palladio's at Bassano
Left The balustrade of the Palladian Bridge

The Ice House here at Prior Park saw a different use during the dark days of World War II. Stocked with ammunition, it would have been manned by resistance fighters if the Germans had invaded. This history only recently came to light when Mr W. G. Dennis wrote to us about his covert wartime activities: 'Patrols of seven men, very well-armed and trained and supplied with substantial quantities of explosives and other devices, would have gone underground if the German army had landed over here. Our job would have been to harass and sabotage their supply lines.'

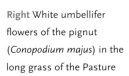

THE PASTURE

For those that want to extend their stay and to experience another aspect of the garden, this pleasant pastoral perambulation offers a taste of the countryside just miles from the city of Bath.

The Horseshoe Walk

At the top of the steps a short detour can be taken into the pasture through a kissing gate. This is an original path which can be clearly seen in the Thorpe & Overton plan of 1762. In fact it appears to be the main route for the circuit, as it is difficult to discern any paths around the Lakes at all. It offers some dramatic views of the bridge from different angles.

Either exit by the gate adjacent to Fishponds Cottage, returning to the city along the pleasant Church Lane, or follow the path beyond the bridge and up the steps.

The Return

The Return is a long zig-zagging route back to the entrance. Notice what a gradual incline this path takes. It has been suggested that a siding

Right White umbellifer flowers of the pignut (*Conopodium majus*) in the long grass of the Pasture

off the main railway, which ran down the hill from the mines, was installed here to allow stone to be transported to build the bridge.

The Rock Gate

Built around 1753, this unusual feature shows experimentation with another style of architecture, this time a sort of Chinese rustic. The mighty 'sponge stones' would have come from the mines, where underground streams flow through limestone seams carving out these curiously shaped rocks in the process. Ralph Allen was happy to share his created landscape and opened Prior Park to visitors on Thursday afternoons, it is likely that this would have been where they entered the garden.

The Rock Gate had almost entirely rotted away by 1993 and craftsmen from the National Trust's building team at Lacock village created this replica.

Turn left and follow the long straight path up the hill. At a point beyond a large beech tree a view opens up to the mansion, the only one from this side of the valley.

Re-entering the Wilderness it is a short walk back to the entrance and starting point.

Below The Rock Gate before and after restoration

CONSERVATION GARDENING

Landscape gardens look intentionally natural, but a lot of work goes into keeping things that way. From day one many different people have been involved in the work of transforming the garden. The few full-time staff are far outnumbered by the team of volunteers who freely give their time to help out.

After the initial clearance work, the way in which planting could enhance the scene was considered. There had been no overlay of exotic planting during the years of neglect. Compare this with the wonderful landscape garden at Stourhead. Here an 18th-century design was heavily planted with a range of rhododendrons and conifers through the 19th and early 20th century. Family members joined the craze for planting trees and shrubs, being introduced from all over of the world. Because this did not happen at Prior Park, the decision

was made to only plant species in Britain before Ralph Allen died in 1764.

Planting the past

Much research has been carried out in recent years into the way in which landscape gardens were planted. The commonly held belief was that flowers were banished and grass swept away from houses into parkland of regularly spaced trees. Mark Laird, author of *The Flowering of the Landscape Garden*, has led the investigation and his book has resulted in a re-appraisal of planting styles. Plans for elaborate flower beds and shrubberies have come to light for other gardens of the period. It is likely that these schemes were carried out, but very little evidence remains on the ground. Flower beds and shrubberies, often planted close to the mansion, would have disappeared without trace, unlike the thousands of trees which were planted in the parkland of the wider estate.

In the Wilderness there is much scope for carrying out plantings of trees, shrubs and herbaceous plants to provide year-round interest. Elsewhere, the effect we strive for is fairly natural. Using plants which do well in the limey soil, we create drifts suggestive of how they would look in the wild. A good example of this is the tutsan, a lovely little shrub which has yellow

Below A sketch by Mrs Delany made in 1743 of the Swift and Swans Island in the garden of Delville Garden in Dublin. This is the planting style gardeners at Prior Park are emulating

flowers followed by dark purple berries. It seeds itself freely and looks just right where ever it establishes itself. Ferns and hemp agrimony are wild plants which also fit in well and create the effect of refined naturalism.

In the area of the Lakes, plantations of field maple, yew, beech and hornbeam have helped to create defined spaces between the grass and water. Two shrubberies have been planted in a graduated scheme near Fishponds Cottage, containing species of hypericum, rose, periwinkle, rubus, lilac and strawberry tree.

Setting the scene

In any garden plants grow, reach maturity and die. This process must be managed to prevent certain species predominating, and this is especially true of laurel at Prior Park. Left unchecked it will soon grow and spread. It is an annual task to prune it and this is carried out in such a way as to leave it looking natural. Growing even in shady areas, it is a good plant for creating effects of light and shade.

Landscape gardens can be seen as stage sets where scenes change and different moods are evoked. From gloomy, inward-looking plantings of evergreens to wide, open vistas, scenes can be contrived to look a certain way. Views to the eye-catchers can also be framed by careful pruning.

Shrubs and trees need careful management: when planted at the same time they tend to mature together. As they mature, they can become lank with bare lower stems. A programme of pruning or cutting them to the ground (coppicing) can prolong the period where they look their best. What is needed are plants at all stages of development so that there are always replacements when large specimens are lost through old age.

23

Top Hemp agrimony (*Eupatorium cannabinum*)

Above Tutsan (*Hypericum androsaemum*) flowering in a rock crevice

Left Hart's tongue fern (*Asplenium scolopendrium*) growing in the rockface of the Cascade

EVER-CHANGING VIEWS

The National Trust owns and cares for a wide range of historic gardens dating from Tudor times to the 20th century. No garden can ever be frozen in time and it is the management of change which is at the heart of garden conservation.

With formal gardens it is possible to recreate, more or less exactly, original layouts. A box parterre for instance can be laid out and planted as it was. As designs become more informal and natural, then things are not so straightforward. This is especially true of landscape gardens such as Prior Park. These places were made as retreats, other worlds, where the distinction between man and nature was deliberately blurred.

Aesthetic sensibilities could be given full rein, and the beauty of nature and man's place in its grand scheme explored. There are interesting parallels to be drawn with the present day: to survive whilst reducing his impact on the planet, man must realise that he is a part of, not separate from, nature. Whatever the changing philosophies at work behind garden-making and conservation, the delights to be found therein remain constant. Gardens are a treat for all the senses, ever-changing through the day, weeks and seasons. It is these immediate pleasures which make garden-making and visiting so rewarding.